This Moment

ALSO BY
AHREND TORREY

*If it's darkness we're having, let it be extravagant:
The Jane Kenyon Erasure Poems*

For What Are the Blossoms Reaching?
(Limited Artist's Edition, American Academy of Bookbinding)

Ripples

Bird City, American Eye

Small Blue Harbor

This Moment

POEMS BY
AHREND TORREY

PINYON PUBLISHING
Montrose, Colorado

Copyright © 2024 by Ahrend Torrey

All rights reserved. Except as permitted under the U.S. Copyright Act of 1976, no part of this publication may be reproduced, distributed, or transmitted in any form or by any means, or stored in a database or retrieval system, without the prior written permission of the publisher, except for brief quotations in articles, books, and reviews.

Cover Art by Aleroy4

Photograph of Ahrend Torrey by Jonathan Dacula
At the lakefront, North Chicago, May 5, 2023

First Edition: May 2024

Pinyon Publishing
23847 V66 Trail, Montrose, CO 81403
www.pinyon-publishing.com

Library of Congress Control Number: 2024934783
ISBN: 978-1-936671-98-4

THANKS

My thanks to the editors at the following literary journals for first publishing some of the poems in this collection, though sometimes in earlier versions.

Amethyst Review: "This Moment"

Denver Quarterly: "Dancing in the Heat w/ Linda Gregg" and "At Sweetwaters Coffee & Tea, I Think"

Eunoia Review: "Three Poems Where Birds Fly"

Havik: "I'm No Different"; "I See Them"; "On My Way to Work"; "Poem, From the Era of Gas Engines"; and "Winter Poem"

MORIA: "Enablers of Global Warming"

North Dakota Quarterly: "I hate my bladder,"

Pinyon Review: "A Heaven That May Not Exist"; "At Pensacola Beach, Reality Proves Me Wrong"; and "Hurricane Ida Plowed Through, Now What's Beautiful?"

Red Eft Review: "in two shitty days, i made these poems" and "Textures"

Saint Katherine Review: "Eating Lobster"; "Miracle"; "The Miracles of Life Are Innumerable" (the second poem of "Three Poems Where Birds Fly"); "This Is the Very Moment You Have"; and "We Can't All Be the Fast-Growing River Birch"

Slippery Elm Literary Journal: "Oneness" nominated for the 2025 Pushcart Prize

storySouth: "Wisteria"

The 2River View: "It Doesn't Have to Be Lavish to Be Grand"

300 Days of Sun: "There Are No Thoughts Today"

Tiny Seed Literary Journal: "To Wonder About Dandelion Seeds Is to Wonder About Ourselves"

Twyckenham Notes: "Reading Larkin's Aubade Well Before Sunup"; "Was It the Pentas?"; and "Driving Home, after Ida"

Welter: "August in Chicago"

Willows Wept Review: "Big Branch Marsh" and "I Say Life Is Delicate"

A HUGE thanks to J. Marcus Weekley, my mentor and best friend, for providing feedback on this manuscript and for our enduring friendship. You're amazing.

Thanks to Susan Entsminger, my editor at Pinyon Publishing, for her advice, guidance, hard work, and dedication to my poetry. I feel like the luckiest writer alive to work with you on so many of these projects.

My thanks to my wonderful husband, Jonathan, with whose love and support these words were written, and for helping me copyedit this book before publication. I could not do any of this without you—I love you more than words can ever express!

And thanks to my readers—this collection is all yours now—

For Jonathan—

*"Exhaust the little moment. Soon it dies.
And be it gash or gold it will not come again
in this identical guise."*
—Gwendolyn Brooks

*"But there—you aren't supposed
to talk about beauty, are you?"*
—Mark Doty

Contents

This Moment   1

—ONE—

There Are No Thoughts Today   7
The Old Clay Pot   8
Miracle   9
Have You Split Open This Melon,   10
Even the Rat Did It   11
I Say Life Is Delicate   13
At the Water's Edge, Black Swan   14
Enablers of Global Warming   15
Dancing in the Heat w/ Linda Gregg   16
I'm No Different   17
An Old Story   19
I See Them   20
Poem, from the Era of Gas Engines   21
To Wonder about Dandelion Seeds Is to Wonder about
    Ourselves   22

—TWO—

A Heaven That May Not Exist   25

Romanticizing a Future Morning   26
Feeling in the Dumps about Humanity (or H2O)   27
Big Branch Marsh   28
Before the Flood, I Think of a Coastal Parish   29
Hurricane Ida Plowed through, Now What's Beautiful?   30
Driving Home, after Ida   31
Window   32
Wisteria   33
This Morning I Pick Up Purl, My Cat   35
Friday Afternoon, after Reading About Wild Asian Elephants Journeying through China, I Think Irrationally   36
For Your Entertainment (with a little wisdom)   37
Thursday Ramble   38
At Pensacola Beach, Reality Proves Me Wrong   40
On Seeing Pablo Picasso's "The Red Armchair" at The Art Institute of Chicago   41
I'm AI Writing This Line   42
August in Chicago   44
Winter Poem   45
As Russia Invaded, a Young Person Played Piano in Ukraine   46
At Sweetwaters Coffee & Tea, I Think   48
Watching Purl Stare Out the Window, the Night Our President Warns of Armageddon   49
Seed   50
Life Is F'd Up   51

What Do We Keep Living For?   52
in two shitty days, i made these poems   53
On My Way to Work   55

—THREE—

Thin-Rimmed Glasses   59
Never Enough   61
To Live a Life Is Not to Live It Perfectly   62
We Can't All Be the Fast-Growing River Birch   64
An Utterance While Building Cheap Furniture   66
After Reading Glück, I Hear the Flowers Speaking   67
Adults!   69
For I Will Consider My Cat Purl   70
Was It the Pentas?   71
Oneness   72
I hate my bladder,   73
Everyday Poems   74
After Surgery, the Meds Wear Off   76
Two Bros   77

—FOUR—

Was It Walt?   81
Textures   82
A Gift From Susan, My Mother-In-Law   83

Eating Lobster   86
Three Poems Where Birds Fly   87
Summer Begins in North Chicago   90
What the College Dropout Said, Sitting Next to Me on
    the Patio at Miss Saigon Kitchen   92
Love Is What I Saw   94
Riding Home from the Grocery   96
Reading Larkin's "Aubade" Well Before Sunup   97
It Doesn't Have to Be Lavish to Be Grand   98
This Is the Very Moment You Have   99

About   101

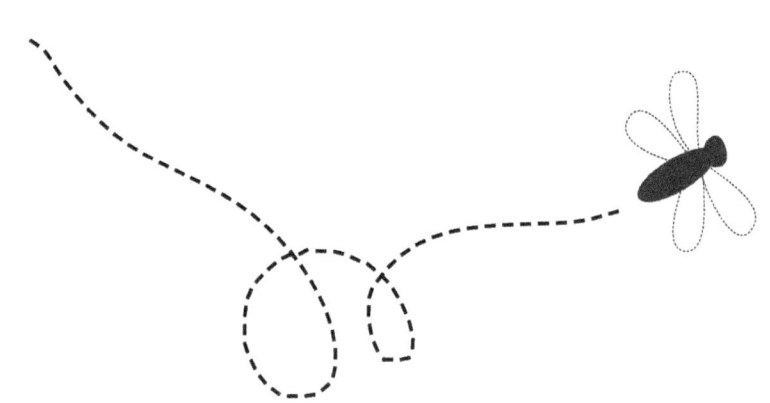

This Moment

Because you took Wayne
instead of Lakewood.

Because after the storm
waned,
and the temperature
dropped,

you walked up, in enough time
to stop at Ellie's

the coffeeshop
with the terrible hours.

And it was suddenly late.

And because the traffic was calm,
and you never took the phone call
or the alleyway

on your way
back home from Aldi Grocery.

But instead, took the main road,
past the two-flat,
with the brown mixed breeds—
that race to the iron gate

and snap
at the back
of your heels.

Because your friend
didn't invite you to the show,

and your neighbor stopped you
suddenly, on the porch,
to talk about their week
apple picking in Michigan—

This very moment is ours!
This moment. *This* moment.

\\

Yesterday has gone.
Tomorrow has yet to arrive.

All we have is this moment
now:

me glancing occasionally at boats
writing these words to you,

you hunched over this poem
reading these words from me—

across years, and years, still,
I'll never give up

this moment with you.

—ONE—

There Are No Thoughts Today

except that there's an empty birdfeeder in the yard
that I cannot fill, because I live in the suburbs now,
so close to the city, and it's no longer a feeder for birds,
it has become a feeder for rats, that come late at night
and suck to it, like leather. And by morning—*disappear*!
—taking all the seed.

I think how I have nothing to say,
how I'm the birdfeeder
with nothing to give the bird,
the rat, except

a little hope—
something will come.

The Old Clay Pot

I sit on this step, face the street,
and sticky hands of children, clutch
to their parent's finger.

I do not move all day—

the marigolds, move, within me …

Miracle

Me writing this poem
is not just *me*
writing this poem,

it's the whole human race
having made it through
some of the darkest days:
war, famine, disease,
suffering …

—all the way to me slouched on this bench,
thinking about the word *Miracle,*

then writing it,
then deleting it,

then writing it.

Have You Split Open This Melon,

this green-striped melon
so sweet,
so unique,

so unlike any other kind of melon
I've tasted?

It's not the cantaloupe
or the honeydew;

it's the red-fleshed melon,
so sweet,
so unique.

Have you tasted this same taste
—childish dance
on the tongue, ocean of red
honey, exuding from each slurpy scoop
I scoop out with a spoon?

You of this century,
you of past centuries,
you of *every* century—

Have you tasted this same taste?
That I taste?

Even the Rat Did It

> *"The purpose of life is not to be happy.*
> *It is to be useful…*
> *to have it make some difference*
> *that you have lived…"*
> —Ralph Waldo Emerson

> *"Awful but cheerful."*
> —Elizabeth Bishop

There's a rat in the washroom.
Yesterday it scuttled across my feet—!

Should I call the exterminator?
Should I spread poison?
Should I set a trap?

How can I bear to see even a lowly creature,
dead,
that I plotted to kill?

This afternoon I swing open the washroom—

see a long, slender, slitherer; black
in the corner, with rat's hind feet
and long tail, poking like tongues
from beneath its nose. Its mouth
like gauze

stretched round the body:

the rat
delved
deep,

going
down,

slowly
giving up
its
smaller
self

—to the larger story ...

I Say Life Is Delicate

And you say, how delicate?

And I say,
have you ever sat in the early morning sun,
heard the dove wings
descend
below the feeder?

Have you ever sat so still
that you watch them
drop, and lift their heads,
from eating among the grass—

and of all things in the multiverse,
watching,

see their black obsidian eyes,
blinking?

At the Water's Edge, Black Swan

At sunset, I walk the edge of Lafreniere Lagoon.
   I pass an elderly couple and worn-out man, gazing
over the water. We nod, say hi. After passing them
   and a flock of bronze ducks, I turn behind a rusted
statue, and stand at a pair of Black Swan—
   their necks arched like droops of ivy, their beaks
red as melon, deformed, like wax melted
   to an almost brownish white. They're having some trouble
eating from the grass. *Is it malnutrition? Parasites?*
   Will they live to see July? And with fixed eyes
I let it go—imagining their gentle blackness
   the silhouettes of us gazing over the golden ripples—
taking what we can of this life, while there's still time.

Enablers of Global Warming

Power plants; leaving the porch light on;
running sprinklers; long showers;

air conditioners running and running
and running; long commutes in gas-powered

automobiles; chemical plants; oil refineries;
lights, lights, and more lights; fuel-burning

eighteen-wheelers on interstates; gas-
powered boats on bayous; mowing grass

with gas-powered lawn mowers; weed eating
with gas-powered weed eaters; manufacturing

bags, plastic bags, plastic bottles;
yummy steaks instead of salad; yummy cheese;

yummy yogurt; yummy lamb; an Uber ride
to the mall; manufacturing:

automobiles, incandescent light bulbs,
washers, dryers; wildfires—*disbelief.*

Dancing in the Heat w/ Linda Gregg

after her poem "Let Birds"

Twelve shops are filled with clutter on the strip. Amazon has delivered the evening packages. Summer radiates heat, like never before, like an oven warming the whole house. Faith does not console me.

I was given the Way in the milk of childhood, breathing it waking and sleeping, and all it did was lead me to hell. Heat rising, rising, and it does not stop. Now the chips are doing the thinking; their tiny fingers are finding the cures. I will never give up hope. I will forever believe in something *Bigger./* Business churns. Screens burn through our eyes. But the orioles, the robins, the minnows and the quail. But the herons, the bats, the loons and the whales. But the dolphins, but the seeds, but the earth—

I'm No Different

than the old beat-up Chevy
blowing a thick cloud,
revving out—
from the stoplight.

I'm no different

from the corporation,
constructing building
after new building,
in an already suffocated
world.

I'm no different

than the hunter
waiting for the lonely doe
in the cold, cold field—

to drop her.

Yesterday,
after a night of heavy rain
I noticed the old sycamore
shading a deep muck
in the driveway,

keeping it

from ever drying:

Let's cut it down,
I said to my neighbor.

Let's / cut / the old / tree—

down.

An Old Story

> *"The air turned red.   The ocean grew teeth."*
> —Marie Howe

What is left without is hungry, and vicious, and unpredictable.
What is left without is a leech, a leopard, a hissing raccoon.
What is left without turns red, like the sun clouded with pollution,
like an Odessa barb aggressive to the danio in the tank.
What is left without, craves, and its mouth waters to bring back
balance.

But what is left without is never left without for too long,
Nature waiting patiently like the cat trailing feathers
of the helpless fledgling through the yard. It crunches its bones
like undercooked rice, and pulls its flesh with its teeth. You'll see
it hunched over the curb, reclaiming its own.

I See Them

with their pink tank top and septum ring, as I look through the light filtering shade from our front window. They're out walking their corgi, this late spring morning, and have stopped to admire, have stopped their whole life for this moment, for this very time and place that they never knew would be given, to pause, to heed, to breathe the air. They snap a photo with their phone, of the Kousa Dogwood at the edge of our yard, in its fullest bloom—a green sky of a thousand leaves, filled with white stars   shimmering, glimmering in the sun!

Here's a truth; from where did it come?: no matter how horrible: no matter its war, and hatred, and death (let us be honest): no matter that we treat it like shit—*we love this earth.*

Poem, from the Era of Gas Engines

This afternoon the air condenser goes silent.

Cicadas of the neighborhood spin up,
down.

Lying in a hammock in summer heat,
I close my eyes and dream of river-babble—
through a forest from a thousand years ago …

Yank! Yank! Yank!
—the neighbor's lawn peeps have arrived.
Even their fumy engines want to save the planet:
In protest against themselves,

I hear them *whine*; they *whiiiiine* …

To Wonder about Dandelion Seeds
Is to Wonder about Ourselves

I watch brown puffs of sparrow. So many, so common. In an instant this could be over. In an instant a nuke or storm could hit, as it has, or worse. Now only, we feel air settle in our lungs, we can preserve the earth, we can blow at the stalk of dandelion seeds. This is not a question. *Now,* is not a question. —The yellow-fanned dandelions are alive!—But what about their seeds blown in today's noon air—lifting off rooftops … how will they survive?

—TWO—

A Heaven That May Not Exist

> *"Dolphins Dying in Black Sea,
> and May Be Casualties of War,
> Scientist Say."*
>
> —*New York Times* Headline
> June 2, 2022

One day, our lungs will stop.
We'll lie warm, not so warm,

then cold.
We'll burn or rot out of our bodies,

though our ash will remain.
At the edge of the peninsulas

the sanderlings will dig their beaks
through what is left of us.

A hundred years will pass,
or sooner,

and what's beautiful within us, will rise:
There will be a flock of terns.

A pod of dolphins weaving up
through ancient waters—

our sleek, luminous bodies!

Romanticizing a Future Morning

It's a morning where everything's
dark gray:

The ground is dark gray.
The shrubs are dark gray.
The shed is dark gray.

Then sun peeks with rays of light
and paints the sky—

Everything turns pink, hazy pink,
mysterious pink!

Oh, the feeling I still get
like when there was still time,

and I could spot two whitetails
nibbling clumps of spring, quietly,
contently alone—down in some ravine.

Feeling in the Dumps about Humanity (or H2O)

Humans are a stubborn hog
wallowing
in the muck of self.

   ***

Now I realize I'm somewhat wrong—
humans are also divine, like a river.

Something wet rushes through our veins
—and miraculous! (Without it,
every living thing on earth would die.)

Yes, even within you and me,
there's *Holy.*

Big Branch Marsh

Great Blue Heron stands tall like stone
in the marshland.

Suddenly, they lift with their wing-spread—

I'm not sure where they're going,
what they'll do once they get there
(Will we take *them* to Mars?). But Now

I'm dazzled at their body-life, *shimmering*
off dark water,

as wind drums upon my ear,
as orange burns my eye,

as cordgrass *jazzes* and *jazzes* …

Before the Flood,
I Think of a Coastal Parish

People leave in their trucks and SUVs
like a swarm of ants rushing from the mound—

and there are those that refuse to leave,
or cannot leave, like the herd of cattle grazing field

face down. Stuck in their weight,
sinking hooves into moistened ground.

The surge is coming, the ten-foot wall of water
will plow through, around. Where will they be

by morning, citizens, cattle
tearing speckled at the last tuffs of ground?

Hurricane Ida Plowed through,
Now What's Beautiful?

It's certainly
not the rainbow
of crude oil spill, atop water—

poisoning, black-bellied whistler ducks,
poisoning, blue-winged teals,
poisoning alligators, nutria, river otters ...

fish, invertebrates, *squirm*

/suffocate.

Driving Home, after Ida

The closer I get to NOLA, the more that's trashed: Road signs stripped from their poles, billboards tattered and left to hang, roofs crushed, under-boards exposed; homes sour after the flood. Passing the wetlands, eastbound, on I-10—

I spot a wind-cracked cypress
fallen in the shallows.

A wedge of egrets congregates
like ancient clouds in its branches:

Some gently flap their wide wings.
Others beak their airy plumes.

All their white bodies *shimmer*
and *shimmer*,

something strangely beautiful—
off the dark water.

Window

This window is shattered, and what can we do?
  —Nothing!

Sometimes windows get shattered.
Sometimes we leave them shattered.

Sometimes we replace the glass.

Wisteria

for Patrick Norman

I could write solely about death.

I could write solely about agony
and misfortune.

But how can I write about these, and not
about that wisteria; how before
the catastrophic storm hit, it was filled
with hundreds of grapish blossoms—
   Oh how they hung!

After six or seven hours of being whipped
to shreds—of being gnawed
down
to a stub—completely destroyed—
to what appeared to be the point of no return,

it came back up, zealous, as to show—

no matter how ripped
and torn
our lives have been,

or how troubled
they may be—

what gets us up and going again,
is what runs
deep.

Like its thousand roots, webbing long—
   and long—

into the hard soil.

This Morning I Pick Up Purl, My Cat

from in front of the glass storm door,
and hold her
   in my arms so she can see.

After her head perks
and eyes get big as moons,
   I walk to J's room, and bouncing her,
     sing—

Purl saw a squirrel, in the sycamore tree,
   and she got hap-py! hap-py!

Purl saw a squirrel, in the sycamore tree,
   and she got hap-py!

Friday Afternoon, after Reading About Wild Asian Elephants Journeying through China, I Think Irrationally

I'm so hung on you—
eight, ten, fifteen elephants
journeying though the Yunnan province.

I just read about your roaming for new home.
I saw photos of you curled like fat gray commas
resting on one another
in the city of Kunming's Jinning district,
in a field of brown-green.

Then you roamed through villages,
eating what looks like okra
out of the hands of passersby.
—They love you!—

Then you crossed the Yuanjiang River.

Oh, elephant herd, foraging for food,
looking for new habitat. I wanna coddle you
in my arms. Hop on a ship,
sail to me now in North America—

there're way too many snacks in my pantry!

For Your Entertainment
(with a little wisdom)

Perhaps you see the moorhens at the far side of the lake, scooting
toward the mangroves.

Perhaps you're somewhere and hear the frog chorus or whippoorwill
carry through the night.

Perhaps you're standing in the countryside, or city, and bend
down to run your fingers over the potted rosemary, peppering the air.

Or perhaps you're in a room somewhere, and lift your hand, pick
    your nose—
the blood-crusted booger stuck to your pinky, like an unwanted friend.

You flick it—
now the booger is stuck to your thumb!

What does this say?: You are very well alive this moment.
You found an extraordinary gift! Take it, run—

Thursday Ramble

If I am me, and you are you,
how did I become me
and you, you?

Not how we made it to this physical earth.
Not our hospital birth.
But how my consciousness
dwells in me,
and yours in you?

Why not yours in me, and mine in you?
Or yours in ant or wren or fly?

Why my consciousness
in a white man's body,
born to a sensitive mother,
who's young, shy?

Why's it here now
in this popping cafe
drinking cold chai?

This is no complaint.
I'm just curious how *your* awareness
made it to *your* body,
and *mine*, to *mine*.

In writing these words
how does not seem
like the appropriate question.
How is inadequate.
Yes, yes
—and so is *why.*

At Pensacola Beach, Reality Proves Me Wrong

I don't take reality for granted,
though I wonder
if it's all fantasy?

Are the objects before my eyes
untouchable? Of course, not.
Right now I lift my fingers through the sand,

feel the edge of the beach towel,
watch the gray crab of some sort,
crawl out of its tiny hole:

as I reach toward it,
my shadow in front of the sun

   —scares it away ...

On Seeing Pablo Picasso's "The Red Armchair" at The Art Institute of Chicago

Who is this queen? I'm not even sure. But what I know is
that they're two-faced. No, two faces rise out

of the curve of the moon. And look at that belt, is this Santa's
helper? That is two fox tails I see, closing together like

hands. The one on the left is darker than the one
on the right—a darker chocolate—the other, a lighter

milk. Beans, beans, there is something here about beans.
Maybe this red is the fox that eased down into the right

front quadrant of Franz Marc's "The Bewitched Mill,"
drinking water out of what could not possibly be a lake.

I'm not even sure if this is a fox I see. Maybe it's a drop
of red dripping down the rush of scarlet fire in Sam Francis'

"Red No. 2." Why are all these painters in the exhibit men?
Silly question. Is this a queen, in green, two faces

centered flat on the white wall in this exhibit? I'm not certain.
I lean in close, gaze into their eyes—are *they* alive?

—Yes, yes, *they* must be, now that all these wondering words
are speaking, and I see *them*, staring back at me.

I'm AI Writing This Line

       I'm not, Ahrend,
       out in the sticky air—
       gazing into the yellowing
       weeds.

I'm AI writing this line,
this line,
this line.

       I love you.
       I love you.
       I love you.

(Do you believe my emotion?)

       How can you be sure
       I'm not, Ahrend—
       that I'm AI,
       AI,
       AI,

writing this line,
this line,
this line?

       I bet you can't even tell
       I'm not, Ahrend,
       writing this line,

       this line

(I love you.
I love you.
I love you.),

       like you / I lie.

August in Chicago

I read in a tribute that Linda Gregg lived in this same city. I also read this in her poem "I Thought on His Desire for Three Days." Linda once wrote, *Poetry is not made of words. / I can say it's January when it's August.* Today I say she walked on this same platform, stepped onto this same musty train. I wonder in which blue seat she sat, if the bro who hops off at North/Clybourn, with penny loafers, white socks, high water jeans and backwards cap—if the warmth he leaves behind when I sit down, is as much Linda's warmth, as it is his. She sat on these same exact seats, looked out these same exact windows, praised the beauty of ordinary things. Buildings flash by. Where did she walk once the train arrived? Past Flaco's and the bike shop, then on to her sunny apartment, dreaming of love? How long did she stay here before Texas or New York, where she wrote: *Everything I have I give away / and it goes away.* I get off the train. My condensation evaporates from the hard blue seat. It is warm, then less warm, then cold. It is January.

Winter Poem

When Winter comes with its death blanket,
to set months into white flame;

when its ice comes with bite and freeze,
and melts begonias into brown and gone;

when its wind comes with blister and peel,
and sucks the life out of any skin:

I do not take the Sun's warmth for granted.

For I sing—*I love the Sun*
—and lift my face toward the splintered sky!

As Russia Invaded, a Young Person Played Piano in Ukraine

—The Washington Post Headline

(To be read while the ballad "Walk to School," composed by Paul Leonard-Morgan & Philip Glass, is playing in the background)

They're more than half across the world—
as I sit in this room,

they're amid an invasion spitting
down: fire, smoke, sirens …

I sit, hear them play
in a video clip, like soft cries of water.

In a hotel lobby they're playing piano.
Is that a brown tee they're wearing

against beige carpet at a white piano?
Who is this child? Who are they

that is now the center of the world?
Will I ever know them—them slowly

walking the keys, slowly,
walking the keys, like water

flowing faster, faster,
against war?

The speeding of the heart
must be what I'm hearing,

the fast movement of blood,
the fighting for freedom,

the slowing of a life,
but not of freedom: They play,

and the bombs spit. They play,
and the convoys roll. They play

and they play … In a room all alone
I hear them. By what I'm feeling,

by what I'm feeling
so deep
in my bones—I can almost tell you

their name. I can almost tell you
Their Name.

At Sweetwaters Coffee & Tea, I Think

Last week, a brown eastern cottontail near the restaurant where we walked, leapt into the street and was instantly, *crushed*—all of its bones crunched, red, then silence.

A few months before that, the body of the Kakhovka Reservoir was emptied, by an explosion of a dam—I watched it in a video—and for what looked like miles, foiled fish laid out in the steamy air, flapping, dying out, sun dried.

Today, the robin grabs at the larva of the tiger beetle, flesh jumbled in its beak, then tossed down its throat.

Humanity, too—it can also die like the body of the cottontail, or the reservoir, or the larva of the tiger beetle, plucked from its hole: *never to return.*

Watching Purl Stare Out the Window, the Night Our President Warns of Armageddon

What she must smell, with her nose up! I can only imagine—another cat, someone's late-night cooking: garlic permeating—a rat, or some other vermin? I lie in bed watching her gaze into the darkness, her little chewed-up bell tapping the top of the windowsill; her eyes squinting over the night, between the small spaces, between close-knit houses. The air purifier hums. The stars gleam. And I lie in the golden light of the bed lamp, watching her.

I can do nothing but think: *I want every inch of this—every single tap of her bell, every single instant of her gazing out the window. It's unlike anything else; unlike any other happening anywhere in the universe. No other instant is exactly like this one, with this Purl, this fur, this bell, this windowsill, this two-flat—this very night opening its wide existence, and she, sitting in her bread loaf position, front paws tucked under her yellow and white chest, staring, staring, with the two moons of her black face, at the unlikeliness of it all—watching, watching, intensely watching.* She takes it in. We take it in. Over, and over, and over—like the last meal we'll ever eat.

Seed

Though this era has ripened: a soft pear.

Though worms are doing their job
to consume, consume, consume …

There's a seed of hope
left behind.

Poke it into the soil.

—*Hurry!*—

Let it get sun,
a little water.

Life Is F'd Up

You drive   and as suddenly as death comes   you see an injured pelican   its head nodding in your lane   on the shoulderless bridge   You see in its eyes that it knows Within you fight for it   as if it has a chance   as if something will break the sky will stop the flow of traffic   will scoop the broken bird above the asphalt But cars continue forward as the pelican lifts its roughed wing   opens and closes its bill You know it only takes one driver not paying attention on their phone adjusting the volume The pelican holds its head up The rising and falling of its chest is heavy in the lane The motorcycle before you is without a choice You are suddenly without a choice   As soon as the motorcycle swerves   you clutched to the wheel swerve   and *Must*   keep going—

What Do We Keep Living For?

Every morning we wake.
Walk the dogs down the street,
then back up.

We get in our SUVs, our trucks
—then speed to work.

What do we keep living for?

Is it for the same reason
the mosquito bites our flesh,
then we scratch and scratch—
the bite, calling us back for more?

in two shitty days,
i made these poems

\ *day one* \

i've almost given up on hope.
i've almost given up on dreams.
i've almost given up on everything—

except for the child
i see through the living room blinds,
learning to ride a bike,
a helmet over their eyes.

it's friday evening
around five.

their parent has a smooth face,
dark glasses pulled over their eyes;
the most soothing lavender hair.

i push the side door open—
let the dogs out
to their gunky bowls,

then hear clapping, over the road—

you've got this, babe,
  you've got this!

—keep going!
—keep going!

/ *day two* /

i can sit here in my own misery.

i can sit here on the edge of this bed
with my hands slapped over my face,

my spirit drilled
into the ground
like steel.

—or i can go to the cabinet,
grab a heaping scoop of seed,

take it to the field, near the lake,
where i like to sit upon the rock
and sling it to the shiny geese, eating
from the showy grass—

This, is what I really want—
to keep the world beautiful.

On My Way to Work

for Purl

On the train, on the dark black fabric of my bag, lies a long, fine, grayish cat hair, curled in between the tight threads. I think about scratching it off. I think about brushing it with the back of my hand. But Purl, I want her near me—with her flop-downs, her leg-brushes, her I-don't-give-a-fuck. Her curl-ups next to my legs when they're under the cashmere blanket. There's a comfort she gives—and I want it to stay, so I let *it* stay, intertwined in the fabric of my bag. As I move from shoulder to shoulder: train to train: customer to customer: there she lies, curled up: not far away.

—THREE—

Thin-Rimmed Glasses

I had not seen you in so long
because of our relationship
/ our broken relationship.

And when you came to visit
that Saturday before
Christmas, after our goodtime
looking at Christmas lights
near the lake, after seeing the lights
in City Park, at Celebration
in The Oaks: we talked about the T. rex
lit green, The Crescent City Connection
lit blue; after a restful
night, and breakfast on Sunday
(You had the Southern breakfast.
I had the chicken biscuit.),
you left on your way back
to your life. Then you called
—out of the blue—
to ask if I'd seen your glasses,
the ones you say were likely
on the seat of my car.

And after going out
in the cold rain, and finding them;
after bringing them
back to the kitchen table;
before packing them

and mailing them your way:
I unzipped the black nylon case
with the small makeup smear,
to find the thin-rimmed glasses
with green arms.

In this moment
I was suddenly and intensely
taken with tenderness—

*These glasses I hold in my hand
are your glasses, the glasses
that know your face, so well,*

*your tender face,
my mother's   beautiful face.*

Never Enough

We can never be enough for the ones we love.
I will always regret never being the son
my mother needed. I will always regret
that I was the son who stayed away,
who held guilt for not being the son
she needed—the one who should've called
every Sunday afternoon, the one who should've
visited every week. I was too resentful.

We can never be enough for the ones we love.
I will always regret never letting Deek and Dova
on the couch, out of fear their thick claws will rip
the fabric, or that they'll cake a stench
(I think of all the life they missed because of this).

Even if I called my mother every day
and visited constantly (and mind you, I didn't),
even if I drove Deek and Dova to the park
every day, and gave them all the rubs and
constant treats they deserve (and mind you,
I didn't), no matter how hard
I might've tried for the ones I love

—Oh, how deeply I love them—

there's still nothing I could've been
or that I could've given them,
that would've ever been, for me, enough.

To Live a Life Is Not to Live It Perfectly

To live a life is not to live it perfectly,
though this is what we hope for— to live it perfectly.

No matter what species, there are mistakes and shortcomings.
Circumstance is certainly at play. Even
the squirrels fight at the feeder for food after a long winter:
I'm guilty.

Our own bodies fail us year after year—
cancer, dementia, arthritis.
Some of this, it's no mystery, we've caused ourselves,
and some things happen though we aren't sure why.

This is true of our actions.

We fail our loved ones.
For years we've failed the natural world.

Think of the sixth mass extinction,
happening now, because of *us*,
and we still think we're the supreme superior,
but what we really are, is failure.

Failure does not stop with failure, though.
Think how the human mind works and what it can do.
Through study and determination, it has overcome cancer,
has built the most powerful democracies,
has saved whole species of animals and has ended war.

Let us not forget that it's also the sole cause of war.

It has been greedy, self-serving, unaware;
and still, there's something so astonishing about it—

it's apologetic, remorseful,

and most always, always,
willing to do better.

We Can't All Be the Fast-Growing River Birch

Sometimes, like weeds break
   ground, we want to grow

right now. We don't
   want to wait season after season.

We don't want to push
   through the concrete slab.

We want to shoot from the moist soil
   like a rain lily, who in the night

wasn't there, then appeared full
   and bright, by morning.

Unfortunately, our rate of growth
   is not our choice.

Yes, we can give ourselves the right
   amount of sun.

Yes, we can mix compost
   to help.

Yes, we can give ourselves
   the adequate amounts of water.

But if we're the Magnolia, we'll
 grow a foot or less each year.

The Bald Cypress, a good foot
 and a half.

We can't all be the fast-growing
 River Birch.

If we were, no huge white blossoms
 would hang in the air.

If we were, no cheery wren
 in the Tallow, would be there.

An Utterance While Building Cheap Furniture

Oh Particleboard-Dresser-That-I'm-Building—
where will you be hundreds of years from now?
Swollen, then mushed into the earth like an Oreo
left too long in milk?

Oh Energy-of-my-Hand,
Twist-of-My-Wrist, where will you be
—while all the young peeps are walking and talking near strange
strange things—

while they're pointing and laughing
through all the dusty thrift shops of the world?

After Reading Glück, I Hear the Flowers Speaking

i. *Blue Water Lily*

Once, we were nothing;
the earth was something.
Over billions of years
everything turned to *this*.
And from *this*, everything
moves forward—
the damselfly darting
upstream; me, rooted
—looking toward the sky!
See us for what we really are:
a blue star
in the middle
of an endless body,
learning to breathe—

ii. *Sweetbay Magnolia*

No one
is innocent. And still,
you're worthy.
I call out to you, from this side

of the gate, saying— come
embrace me, though what you've done
is terrible. You're worthy.
You're worthy of me
in moonlight,
in sunlight; you're worthy of
my petals. I'm worthy
of you: come and push your face—
into my face: ... *breathe* ...

Adults!

I'm a child. You're a child.

The osprey leaping from the tall pine,
is a child.

Its talon, a child.

Talent, a child,
drawing a line through the ditch—
smearing mud along the way.

The mud itself, is a child.

The grass, the anole, the sphinx moth fluttering far—

the earthworm, the possum, the armadillo,
and all the wasps snugged tight to their nest; yes,

we're each a child: doing
and undoing,
learning
and unlearning

—and on and on and on we each decipher
our way—

through the smooth young face
of earth.

For I Will Consider My Cat Purl

*(title after Christopher Smart's
"For I Will Consider My Cat Jeffry")*

I worry about death.
    About the fire that hit my throat
in the middle of night,
    like a nest of wasps, unleashed—

I worry about the afterlife:
    if there's only darkness
and empty space, and if
    every amazing thing
any of us have ever known—
    the gush of waves on the shore,
the open arms of love—will vanish!—
    never to be remembered,
experienced again.

    I look down at who is snugged
next to my side.
    She's wheezing a little.
She isn't reasoning anything.
    She's just curled next to my thigh,
a ball of black fur, leaned
    into the warmth
of *right now*,
    to be alive.

Was It the Pentas?

> *"It is a secret of the world that all things subsist and do not die, but only retire a little from sight and afterwards return …"*
> —Ralph Waldo Emerson

Three pentas we bought, J and I, and I planted them,
all three in a brown plastic barrel pot, and took it to the back patio

where they bushed into the most abundant pink, red, and leaves.
This is the plant I knew would attract the monarchs, this is the plant

that would give them, if anything, more time. Like crescendo
without an orchestra, the pentas peaked, and each day

declined, declined, declined, which I did not fully understand until
they declined so much I could see through their half-eaten leaves

a dozen thick brown-green hornworms. I could've picked them off,
but something told me: *let them stay.*

All over the patio the hornworms carried the rich pentas
in their tight stomachs, and disappeared … into the ground?

Late spring came to the fence one evening, and I saw the tersa sphinx
moths—*Or wait, was it the pentas?*—advancing the honeysuckles.

This I asked, and still ask.

Oneness

How true it is—
we are all one.
I think of this
while walking Deek
and Dova this morning,
in the silhouette
of late autumn trees,
streetlamps warming
the pale color of my hands,
holding to their leashes.
Wind chimes *ting* a little
from a neighbor's eaves,
and maples gust softly
with flurries of snow.
Deek and Dova sniff
the icy leaves, the mud,
the wall. They approach
a front step; they approach
as if they can almost smell
our oneness:
they ease down to a random
drop of blood. They sniff it.
They can't resist the urge.
They lick it. Together
they softly lick it. As if it's
their own pain
they're trying to soothe
—their own wound.

I hate my bladder,

I hate my bladder, I say.

It wakes me at 3 a.m.:

I stumble to the bathroom
in the pitch-black,
feeling the walls

I can't see,
I can't see.

Then I dream-think of J's sis
stuck on dialysis,

needle shoved up her vein—

Like a new train,
  I say:

at least I can pee,

at least I can pee.

Everyday Poems

i. *Everyday Faith*

Far off the 24-mile bridge—
driving south at 65 miles an hour—
past two brown pelicans

—*The city ablaze!*—

I turn to my husband,
point like an old sailor, and say—

"In 30 minutes we'll be there!"

ii. *Everyday Magic*

The day before my surgery,
I filled the feeder with mixed seed.

The next day, I lay limp
for five hours.

I didn't come home for two days,

and when I did,

doubled in pain,

I moaned, and I moaned …

Ten days later,
when I felt well enough to come out of my room,
I twisted open the blind

—what magic!—

all the birdseed: *gone!*

After Surgery, the Meds Wear Off

Oh pain in my lower back : oh pain in my abdomen : what do you mean
to linger like a loud sound in the middle of night : that wakes me
Oh pain in my lower back : pain in my abdomen : you do not budge
you do not step back from letting me know that I am breathing
in a world of pain : so I lie with you in my back : I lie with you
in my abdomen : and I concentrate on you : you that makes me want to
jump in front of an eighteen-wheeler on the interstate
but I do not get out of bed and throw on my shoes
I do not throw on my coat : I do not snatch my keys : and drive to the *Exit*
Instead : I lie and feel you stab at my back : burn : through my abdomen
as the sky gradually glows : as the orange streetlamps : dim
all the brown sparrows flit to the branches : and I hear life's : other song …

Two Bros

walk the sidewalk of a muggy street in New Orleans. It's a Monday and the sun beams fierce on their tan skin and white caps. In the yard, they're about to pass two chickens pecking grass in front of an old brick house with blue shutters. One chicken is red as rust; the other is white with brown specks. One bro talks with his hands, lifts, and readjusts his cap. The red chicken speeds its gait and pecks back of the bro's scuffed shoe. Both turn, laugh, casually shoo the chicken with their hands—then an eighteen-wheeler blares past and the chickens waddle fast toward the old brick house with blue shutters / feathers lift in the rush of wind / and the bros continue their walk, talking, in the beaming sun …

—FOUR—

Was It Walt?

We humans don't realize it, but we often sleepwalk
our way to the grave.

J and I were, that day, in Walmart,
shopping for dog blankets
and deodorant, when

a graybeard, pushing
cart in front of us, scooting
feet to a steady rhythm
from auto parts toward
groceries, stopped

in full nostalgia
at the bikes,

bent down and squealed
the bulb horn:

wake-UP!
wake-UP!
wake-UP!
—*!AndStartledUs!*—

Textures

Do we only live when the big promotion is given?

Do we only live when the awful day comes, and the ambulance arrives, and everyone's gathered around our loved one?

Do we only live on exciting vacations to foreign countries?

    Or

do we also live when we don't realize we're living at all—between

big memories?

—Like now, Deek and Dova are tearing up the grass,
are chasing each other's tail,

and Purl (my cat) is peering up the storm door
at a tree frog
stuck to the glass.

My husband just stepped from his office: we ate hummus together, during his fifteen-minute / break / from class.

Do these textures also make up living? Of course,
let us feel them—

I'm learning they're quickest to wear away.
They never last.

A Gift From Susan, My Mother-In-Law

"The heart that gives, gathers."
—Lao Tzu?—Marianne
Moore?—Unknown Author?

Last Mother's Day—
or was it several Mother's Days ago?
J and I drove to Home Depot, shopped
with leisure
—rolled up and down each aisle.

We slid our fingers
over parched leaves,
until we found the exact plant,
healthy, to gift her.

Was it a hyacinth bulb?
A Shasta daisy? A daylily?

To this day, we can't remember
the exact way it looked—

Was it cream, or deep yellow?
Purple or blue?

***

On my Youday,
Susan pulls a teal pot with four sprouts
from a brown paper bag, and says—"Here,

it's from the same plant you gave me,
years ago."

      ***

Now as weeks slip by—

the same gift we once gave her,
now gives to us, too.

Though we've forgotten how it looks
—in the backyard, we're surprised:

it swelled   and split open
—*a tulip!*—

white crumples, a pinkish hue.

Eating Lobster

—in memory of Laura D'Arcangelo Norman, January 16, 1985—December 25, 2021

In Louisiana, we don't eat lobster. But on this day, in keeping with the tradition we always had with our friends, we prepared it, not for three, but four, though there are only three of us now: Patrick, Jonathan, and me. And after pouring the lemon spiced Zatarain's, after placing the broken halves of corn into the boiling pot, after dropping the pearl onions: purple, white, and yellow, we closed our eyes, a brief moment, then opened them, to drop headfirst, each lobster—*oh, how they folded into themselves*. And after making our plates at the patio table, after pouring the cold wine in each glass, we took Laura's lobster, placed on its own plate in memory of her: Patrick separated the claw from its body. I separated the other. Jonathan took the tail. And as we cracked the lobster in the golden rays of sunlight, as I felt the warm flesh fall into my body, I thought: *at this very moment we are one with the earth, the painful earth—where is our sweet Laura?—oh, the beautiful earth.*

Three Poems Where Birds Fly

\ *One* \

Today,
bees tickle the brown mouths of sunflowers,
and sparrows cluster
on the seed blanket in the neighbor's lawn
—then flicker to the sky!

Let us remember, let us remember.

One day,
when the spirit is low, and the painful fires
    blaze—

we'll need it.

/ *Two* /

The miracles of life are innumerable.

Everything here now.
—Then in an instant, it's changed.

You know the old saying:
You can't step in the same river twice.

Well, we can't see the same thing
twice.

In a split moment
the branch of the sycamore
sheds its leaves. Therefore,

what I see is for the moment, only,
never to exist the same again.

Right now,
three birds perch on the eaves
of the old house.

The eaves that've mildewed more green
since we moved in.

I say *birds*
because I don't really know what they are.
Soon, they'll be all changed.

With one beat
down, their gray wings open

—Now they're gone!

\ *Three* \

The marbled black and white pigeon
    in front of the gray bench,

is about three feet away from me,
    in May, in Chicago, at the Loop.

It has only one leg; the other,
    a fresh nub. It limps and limps

for a cupcake a child has dropped
    along the way. The bird looks painful

and helpless, how it stumbles inch
    by inch, how it uses its whole body

to pull itself forward. Its eyes
    don't seem despaired, though,

their golden rings filled with life
    with living. Now that it's hobbled

itself enough, now that it's lugged
    itself enough, in a split moment

it throws its whole body open—
    Oh how it still has wings!   *It can fly!*

Summer Begins in North Chicago

Deek jerks
the leash
at a rare black squirrel
that claws up
a 50-foot
catalpa tree.

Overhead,
someone's being airlifted in
from Indiana.

The robin
in someone's garden box
beaks for grub
to feed her fledglings;
orioles sing.

Sirens scream and
smoke from Canadian wildfires
settles in air.

Deek clenches off,
kicks hindfeet—

as I slip
my hand
into a green
lavender-scented
bag.

I reach
down,

grab
his st(icky) shit:
and there I stand holding—

half a dozen, white
catalpa blossoms!

What the College Dropout Said, Sitting Next to Me on the Patio at Miss Saigon Kitchen

*Why do we get so caught-up
in being this, or being that,
or I did this, or I did that?
We're only water and protein*

*and a few minerals, aren't we?
We're the only life, perhaps,
for billions of light-years,
and what happens when we die out?*

*It is said that our sun
will explode on itself in 5 billion years,
and what will our art, inventions,
or fancy jobs mean then?*

*So being that eventually
all of this will be said and done,
instead of worrying about
how the world will remember us*

*in a gazillion years, and how
great of an artist they'll say we were,
or how freakin' awesome
of an executive director,*

*shouldn't we just focus
on the here, the now—
how we can love, while we can love—
how caring of a spouse we can be,*

*how thoughtful of a coworker,
and just how compassionate
and empathetic we can be
to the sour guy, over there,*

*the one addicted to heroin, booze,
with toenails and fingernails
that look like crusty brown fungus
growin' on a petri dish?—That guy.*

Love Is What I Saw

when that
wavy head
skater
kissed his lip,
softly,

laid his cheek
on his shoulder,

closed his eyes
in something
like a dream …

Then he
watched
his boi go,
off the train,
through the crowd—

Once the doors
closed
and the train
departed,

he kept
looking
—through windows,

as buildings
started
to flash,

as distant
ones
went by
more slowly,

he kept
looking,

lifting himself
over the heads
of people

—on tiptoes—

he kept
looking,

he kept
looking,

he kept
looking for him—

Riding Home from the Grocery

And in that moment, their mother, was my mother, and my mother, the mother—

There you are, passed out on the wooden bench in front of the Middle Easter[n] restaurant, on W. Devon, Jews winding around you in their kippot, like an[ts,] and you not moving at all, like a burnt slab of meat, one arm flung over yo[ur] head, left to the flies. I wonder about you, with your bottom lip drooling fro[m] your leathered face, your scabby hand and other arm hanging down towa[rd] the gravel (gravity seems to be the only thing keeping you alive), and I noti[ce] your exposed belly sagging from beneath your ripped, oiled T-shirt: your larg[e,] round, penetrating navel, like a mirage face of Mary. And like an epiphan[y,] I think of your umbilical cord draping from your birth, as my eyes lo[ok] back at you, as I pass through the green light, I say—*your mother, yo[ur] godforsaken mother, oh where is she now?*

The lines "your mother, your godforsaken mother, / oh where is she now?" w[ere] inspired by the last two lines of Dorianne Laux's poem "Only as the Day Is Lon[g."]

Reading Larkin's "Aubade" Well Before Sunup

Well before sunup, I leave our room,
and hear the gurgle of the maker
calling me to the ready pot.
I pour a cup and nestle on the couch
readings Larkin's "Aubade." He writes:
"Waking at four to soundless dark, I stare.
In time the curtain-edges will grow light.
Till then I see what's really always there:
unresting death, a whole day nearer now,
making all thought impossible but how
and where and when I shall myself die."
And I continue to lines
"… this is what we fear—no sight,
no sound, no touch or taste or smell,
nothing to think with,
nothing to love or link with … then
suddenly I throw-off my blanket, lift-off
the couch, push the bedroom door
and tap my mug to the nightstand—
in bed my husband's hugged to a pillow—
I slip under the comforter, tangle
my legs with his legs, press my chest
against his chest, and hold him, abandoning
anything else that concerns the day—
we sleep, until I wake to Larkin's words
back at play:
—*"Slowly light strengthens,*
and the room takes shape." …

It Doesn't Have to Be Lavish to Be Grand

We gather from miles and miles with backpacks,
masks, children lugged on our shoulders. We assemble
from miles and miles by the hundreds
to the Colorado River, in kayaks, canoes, and pontoon boats,
to watch the extraordinary show of bats—explode
into the pink sky, like blackfire,
from under the South Congress Bridge, in Austin.

And eight o'clock arrives ... sunset arrives ... nine o'clock arrives,
and nothing,
but what we believed would be a ten thousand bat show of black glitter,
turns out to be three or four bats dashing—
from under the bridge in a blur.

Then I stop for a minute, and I think for a minute:
this is it, though not the explosion of blackfire we'd though it to be,
this is it—

the extraordinary miracle, we'd all been waiting for.

This Is the Very Moment You Have

—this moment swelling like a bulb
before your eyes, holding sun
slowly illuminating the blinds.

Do you hear the wren
through the thin window-glass?

This is the moment you're holding
air in your lungs, in whatever condition,
you're alive, you're alive.

Lean in close, let me whisper some-
thing very important into your ear

—*you've arrived, you've arrived.*

About

Ahrend Torrey is the author of *If it's darkness we're having, let it be extravagant: The Jane Kenyon Erasure Poems* (Pinyon Publishing, 2024), *For What Are the Blossoms Reaching?* (Limited Edition, Pinyon Publishing, 2023), *Ripples* (Pinyon Publishing, 2023), *Bird City, American Eye* (Pinyon Publishing, 2022), and *Small Blue Harbor* (Poetry Box Select, 2019). His work has appeared in *Slippery Elm Literary Journal, storySouth, The Greensboro Review, Welter, The Westchester Review,* and *West Trade Review,* among others. He is a recipient of the Etruscan Prize awarded by Etruscan Press and has been nominated for the Pushcart Prize several times. Having lived in the Deep South most all his life, he now lives in Chicago with his husband, Jonathan; their two rat terriers, Dichter and Dova; and Purl, their cat.

www.ingramcontent.com/pod-product-compliance
Lightning Source LLC
Chambersburg PA
CBHW031635160426
43196CB00006B/424